Scout Goes to School

By Barbara Jo Almendinger

Illustrated By Haley A. Thompson

proving
press

Book Design & Production: Columbus Publishing Lab
www.ColumbusPublishingLab.com

Copyright © 2018 by Barbara Jo Almendinger
Illustrated by Haley A. Thompson

LCCN: 2018956615
Paperback ISBN: 978-1-63337-222-1
Hardcover ISBN: 978-1-63337-223-8
E-book ISBN: 978-1-63337-225-2

Printed in the United States of America
1 3 5 7 9 10 8 6 4 2

Every day, Scout Sawyer Shakespeare gets to go to school. She does what she does best—loving every boy and girl at Utica Middle School every single day.

Each morning, Scout races down the hallway, making her rounds.

First stop, Mrs. Bennett for her morning treats, then on to Mrs. Imbody and Mrs. Londot for more treats, and lastly to Mrs. A's classroom to clean up the crumbs from the students' breakfast.

Scout wears many different hats, and not just on hat day. She comforts kids by letting them pet her, she helps them stay calm on test days, and she listens when they need a friend.

Unlike the students in Mrs. A's class, Scout does not get into trouble for sleeping during class.

Scout loves to play kickball outside with Mr. Ballinger's gym class.
Sometimes she gets so excited she bites a hole in the ball, which means
game over for the kids.

Scout most certainly does not like it when there are fire drills, as the loud noises hurt her sensitive doggy ears.

One day, during the fire drill, she got so excited she pulled Mrs. Williams down the stairs. Luckily, everyone was okay.

Scout loves doing tricks for treats. She can sit, stay, shake, high-five, and roll over.

Scout ate so many treats that she could not roll over anymore. That is when Scout had to go on a diet.

One day, Bella gave Scout a kindness card. This made Scout feel special and she wagged her tail even more that day.

Kindness Card

To: Scout

You have been an amazing and wonderful dog! You've helped me get through this school year! You are the best!

From: Karen Lightle

Kindness Card

To: Scout

You are a great dog. Woof. Woof

Kindness Card

To: Scout

you are very cute and are a very sweet dog. I love walking you and seeing you at school :)

From: Bella ♡

11

Scout gets to go outside every day with the kids.

One sunny day, Scout started barking when she saw another dog, or what she thought was another dog, but it was just her own reflection in the glass doors.

Scout loves every one of the 300 plus students at Utica Middle School. She knows when there is a visitor in the building, and often barks at strangers. Stranger danger!

IMBODY

One day Scout was bad, and she left the classroom without permission.

Mrs. Imbody wrote Scout a lunch detention slip. Scout slept through the entire detention.

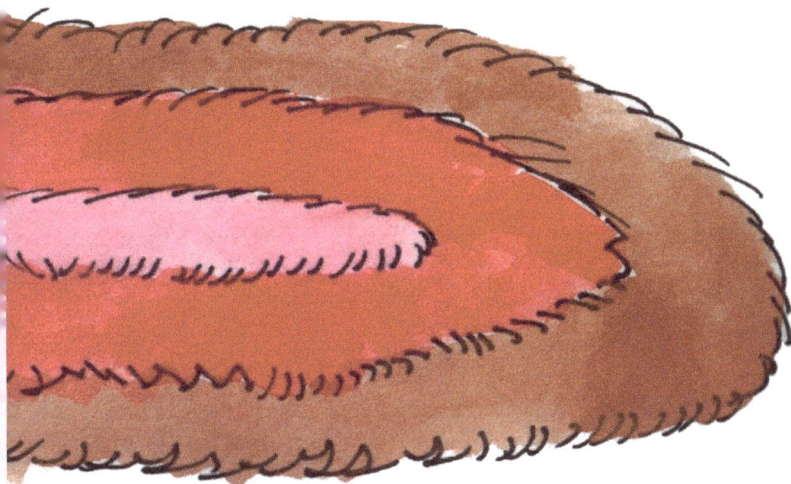

Scout loves to lie down and cross her paws in front of her.
One day Danielle decided she wanted to lay on the floor and cross
her arms, just like Scout.

Scout went missing one day and no one could find her. Mrs. Bennett had to make an announcement, "Scout, please report to the office."

One day in class Mrs. A said, "Students, please make sure your name is on your homework and pass your papers up."

Steven passed up his paper, but Scout jumped up and ate it. Steven immediately raised his hand and said, "Mrs. A., the dog really did eat my homework, I promise."

At the end of especially long days, Scout takes refuge under Mrs. A's desk for a much-needed rest. Sometimes it's a tough job taking care of all the students.

UTICA JUNIOR HIGH SCHOOL
Lunch AFTER SCHOOL DETENTION

Name: Scout

Date of incident: 2.9.18

Teacher: Imbody

[ ] Conference with *student* about this detention

[ ] Conference with *parent* about this detention

Date of detention: 2.9.18

Comments: Left our Classroom without Permission.
Caught Wondering the Halls without hall pass.

Parent's Signature: _____ **Date:** 2.9.18

Copies: White and yellow copies – Student (<u>One is to be returned with parent's signature.</u>)
Pink – Office

DETENTION GUIDELINES

1. After school detentions are held every Wednesday beginning at 2:30 and ending at 3:30.
2. Failure to report to after school detention will result in further disciplinary action.
3. You must bring with you homework, or material to keep yourself busy throughout the entire time.

20

About Scout

Scout Sawyer Shakespeare is a therapy dog at Utica Middle School. She started her career in the classroom in January 2014 when she was just four months old. Scout's first name comes from the book *To Kill a Mockingbird* (my favorite book). Her middle name, Sawyer, comes from the book *The Adventures of Tom Sawyer* (my favorite character in a book). Scout is also named after Shakespeare, the famous poet and playwright.

At school, Scout is used to brighten each student's day, offer emotional support, and be a friend to each student every single day. She is a great listener, and an even better beggar of treats. Scout spends most of her day in Mrs. Almendinger's classroom, being walked by a variety of students, and also laying in the hallways between class changes. This book was written as a tribute to Scout, and dogs everywhere, who just make the world a better place.

About the Author

Barbara Almendinger has been a Utica Middle School language arts teacher for over twenty-six years. She holds a Bachelor of Science in Education from The Ohio State University, and a Master of Science in Education with a concentration in school counseling from Dayton University. In 2012, Barbara was awarded the Leaders for Learning in Education award for her county.

She currently lives in Alexandria, Ohio, with her two sons, David and Jeremy, and their yellow lab, Scout. Scout is a trained therapy dog who accompanies her to school, engaging and inspiring her students to learn. Barbara is passionate about teaching young adults and encouraging them to adopt a lifelong love for reading.

About the Illustrator

Haley A. Thompson was Mrs. Almendinger's student for 8th grade English and language arts in 2013-2014. Haley then went on to high school where she illustrated the *Scout Goes to School* book as her senior year art project. Haley will be attending the Columbus College of Art and Design and will major in Comics and Narrative Practice. Haley is an avid lover of dogs and drawing. She was part of the first class of students to have Scout as a full-time therapy dog.

Scout
&
A Butterfly

This line drawing is the first illustration of Scout that Haley Thompson did as an 8th-grade student in Mrs. Almendinger's class.

~WoTN 2014

www.ingramcontent.com/pod-product-compliance
Lightning Source LLC
Chambersburg PA
CBHW040849100426
42813CB00015B/2755